D1244285

COMMUNITY HELPERS

Plumbers

by Kate Moening

BLASTOFF! READERS

BELLWETHER MEDIA · MINNEAPOLIS, MN

Note to Librarians, Teachers, and Parents:

Blastoff! Readers are carefully developed by literacy experts and combine standards-based content with developmentally appropriate text.

Level 1 provides the most support through repetition of high-frequency words, light text, predictable sentence patterns, and strong visual support.

Level 2 offers early readers a bit more challenge through varied simple sentences, increased text load, and less repetition of high-frequency words.

Level 3 advances early-fluent readers toward fluency through increased text and concept load, less reliance on visuals, longer sentences, and more literary language.

Level 4 builds reading stamina by providing more text per page, increased use of punctuation, greater variation in sentence patterns, and increasingly challenging vocabulary.

Level 5 encourages children to move from "learning to read" to "reading to learn" by providing even more text, varied writing styles, and less familiar topics.

Whichever book is right for your reader, Blastoff! Readers are the perfect books to build confidence and encourage a love of reading that will last a lifetime!

This edition first published in 2019 by Bellwether Media, Inc.

No part of this publication may be reproduced in whole or in part without written permission of the publisher. For information regarding permission, write to Bellwether Media, Inc., Attention: Permissions Department, 6012 Blue Circle Drive, Minnetonka, MN 55343.

Library of Congress Cataloging-in-Publication Data

Names: Moening, Kate, author.
Title: Plumbers / by Kate Moening.
Description: Minneapolis, MN : Bellwether Media, Inc., [2019] | Series: Blastoff! Readers: Community Helpers | Audience: K to Grade 3. | Includes bibliographical references and index.
Identifiers: LCCN 2018030423 (print) | LCCN 2018033581 (ebook) | ISBN 9781681036359 (ebook) | ISBN 9781626179042 (hardcover : alk. paper)
Subjects: LCSH: Plumbing–Vocational guidance–Juvenile literature. | Plumbers–Juvenile literature. | CYAC: Occupations–Juvenile literature.
Classification: LCC TH6124 (ebook) | LCC TH6124 .M64 2019 (print) | DDC 696/.1023–dc23
LC record available at https://lccn.loc.gov/2018030423

Editor: Betsy Rathburn   Designer: Brittany McIntosh

Printed in the United States of America, North Mankato, MN.

Table of Contents

A Leaky Faucet

Uh-oh! The kitchen sink has a **leak**. The plumber will fix it!

The plumber puts
in a new pipe.
The leak stops.
Good as new!

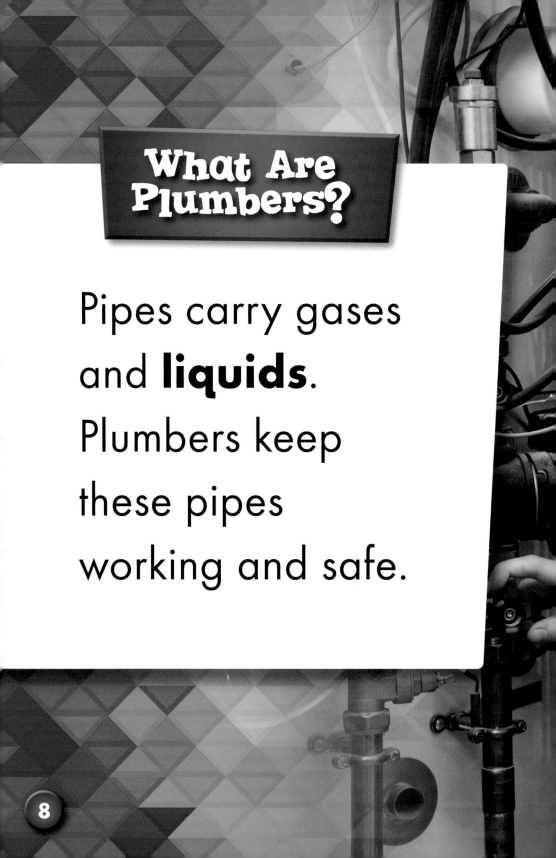

What Are Plumbers?

Pipes carry gases and **liquids**. Plumbers keep these pipes working and safe.

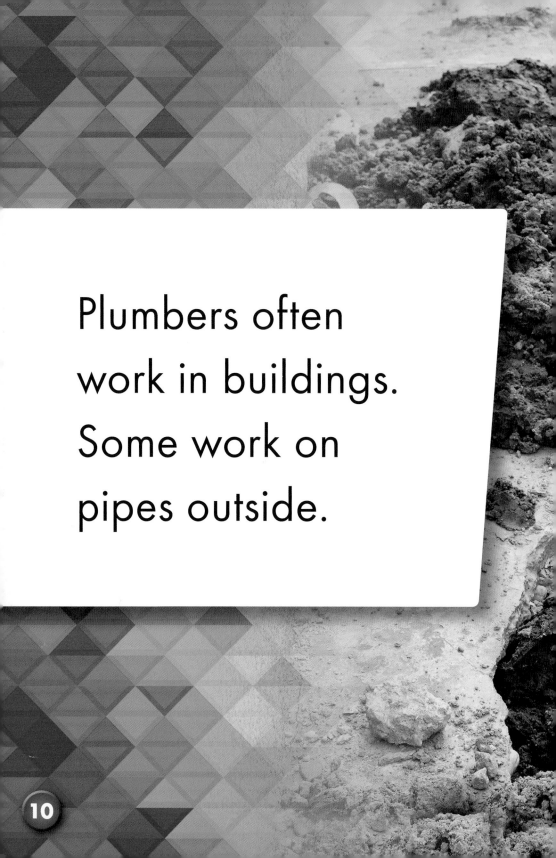

Plumbers often work in buildings. Some work on pipes outside.

What Do Plumbers Do?

Plumbers **install** and test new pipes. They also fix pipes that are worn out.

Some plumbers work on people's homes. They put in toilets, dishwashers, and other **appliances**.

Plumber Gear

wrench　　drill　　welding torch　　gloves

Plumbers must be good listeners. They help people understand problems with pipes.

What Makes a Good Plumber?

Plumbers work on many **projects**. They know which pipe to use for each one!

Plumber Skills

✓ good with their hands ✓ problem-solvers

✓ good with people ✓ strong

Plumbers read **blueprints**. They know where each pipe goes. They keep buildings running!

Glossary

appliances

tools or machines that have special uses

leak

a crack or hole that lets gas or water out

blueprints

maps of buildings that tell plumbers where the pipes are located

liquids

matter that flows freely, such as water

install

to set up for people to use

projects

specific jobs that plumbers work on

To Learn More

AT THE LIBRARY

Leaf, Christina. *Mechanics*. Minneapolis, Minn.: Bellwether Media, 2019.

Meister, Cari. *Plumbers*. Minneapolis, Minn.: Bullfrog Books, 2015.

Rose, Simon. *Plumber*. New York, N.Y.: AV2 by Weigl, 2016.

ON THE WEB

FACTSURFER

Factsurfer.com gives you a safe, fun way to find more information.

1. Go to www.factsurfer.com.

2. Enter "plumbers" into the search box.

3. Click the "Surf" button and select your book cover to see a list of related web sites.

Index